LEFT HANDED
Cursive
HANDWRITING WORKBOOK
FOR KIDS

AGES 6+

 ALPHABETS & NUMBERS  WORDS  SENTENCES

3 PARTS

This workbook is divided into the following parts.

Part 1 : Trace and practice the cursive letters and numbers

Part 2 : Trace and practice simple words

Part 3 : Trace and practice simple sentences

FOR ANY SUGGESTS OR QUESTIONS REGARDING OUR
BOOK, PLEASE CONTACT US AT :
ATNINTHDESSERT@GMAIL.COM

ISBN: 979-8828383047

A Few Helpful Tips

— LEFT-HANDERS —

- Left-handed people should sit slightly to the left of the center and tilt the paper down for better visibility. Therefore, this workbook is designed with slanted lines to prevent getting caught, dirty and improve visibility without tilting.

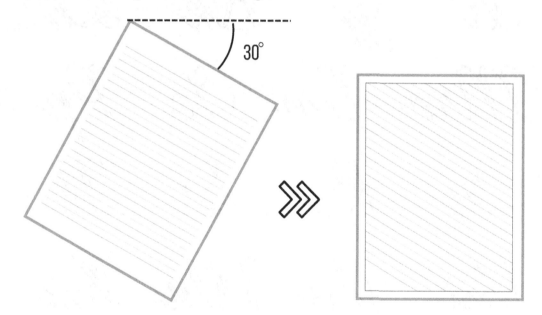

30°

- Left-handed writers should also have enough lighting so that the shadow of your hand doesn't interfere with your writing.

- Left-handed cursive writers should use a pencil grip to hold the pencil far enough away from the tip. This allows you to better see the formation of the letters you are writing on the paper.

Cursive Alphabet Guide

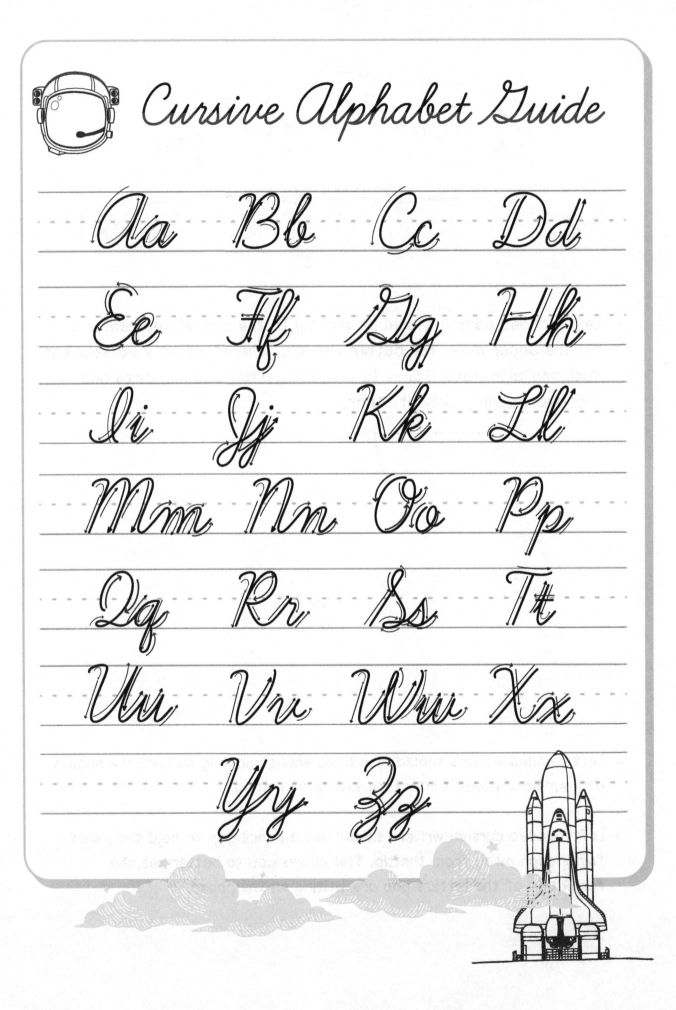

Aa Bb Cc Dd

Ee Ff Gg Hh

Ii Jj Kk Ll

Mm Nn Oo Pp

Qq Rr Ss Tt

Uu Vv Ww Xx

Yy Zz

Part 1

Learn and practice

Alphabets

Cursive letters A-Z and a-z

Numbers

Cursive numbers and
number words 0-9

Can use a pencil, light color markers
to trace the dotted words.

Trace the cursive letters, then write your own.

a is for Ant

Trace the cursive letters, then write your own.

B is for Bear

Trace the cursive letters, then write your own.

C is for camel

Trace the cursive letters, then write your own.

D is for Dolphin

Trace the cursive letters, then write your own.

E is for Elephant

Trace the cursive letters, then write your own.

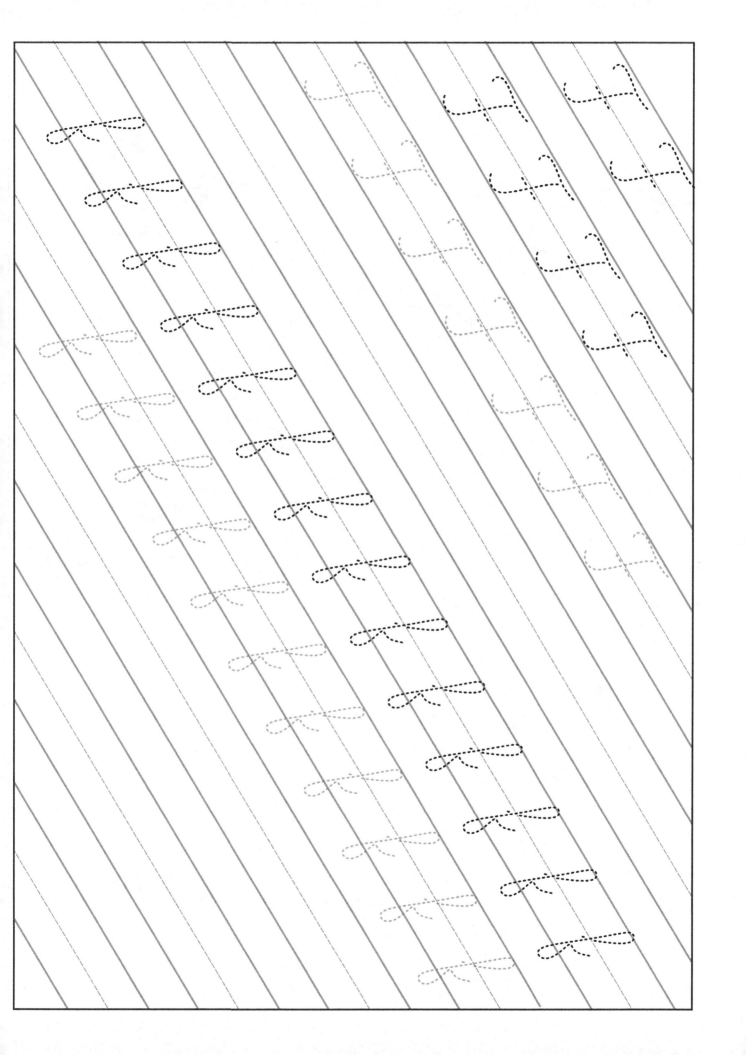

Trace the cursive letters, then write your own.

g is for giraffe

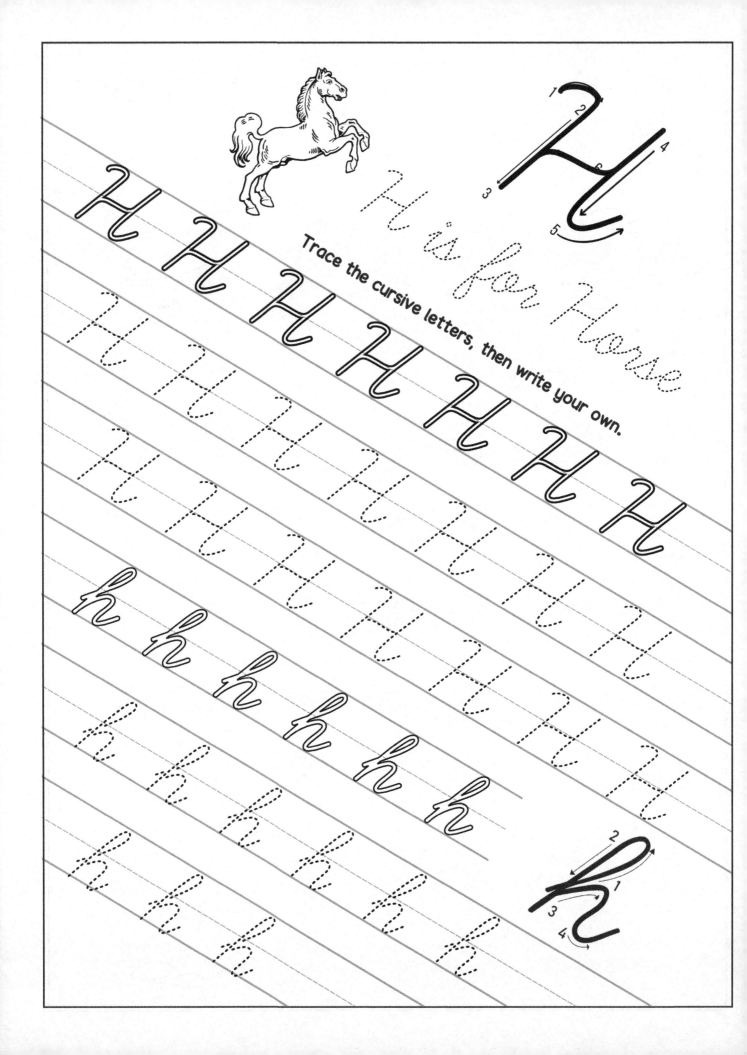

Trace the cursive letters, then write your own.

H is for Horse

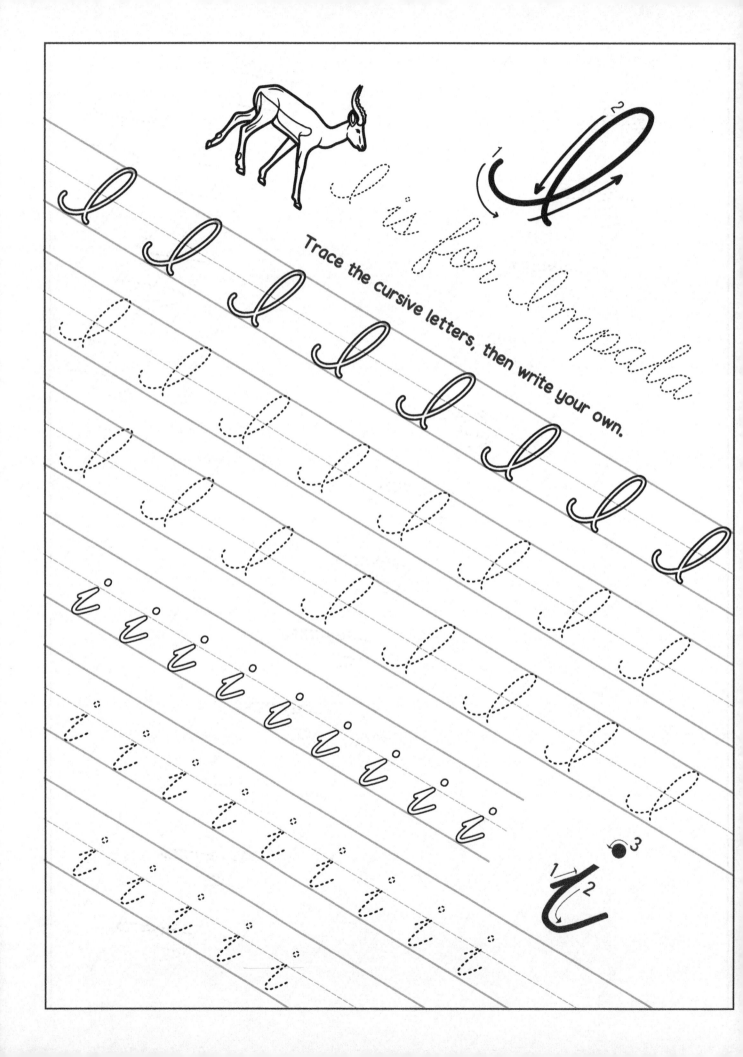

Trace the cursive letters, then write your own.

Trace the cursive letters, then write your own.

J is for jellyfish

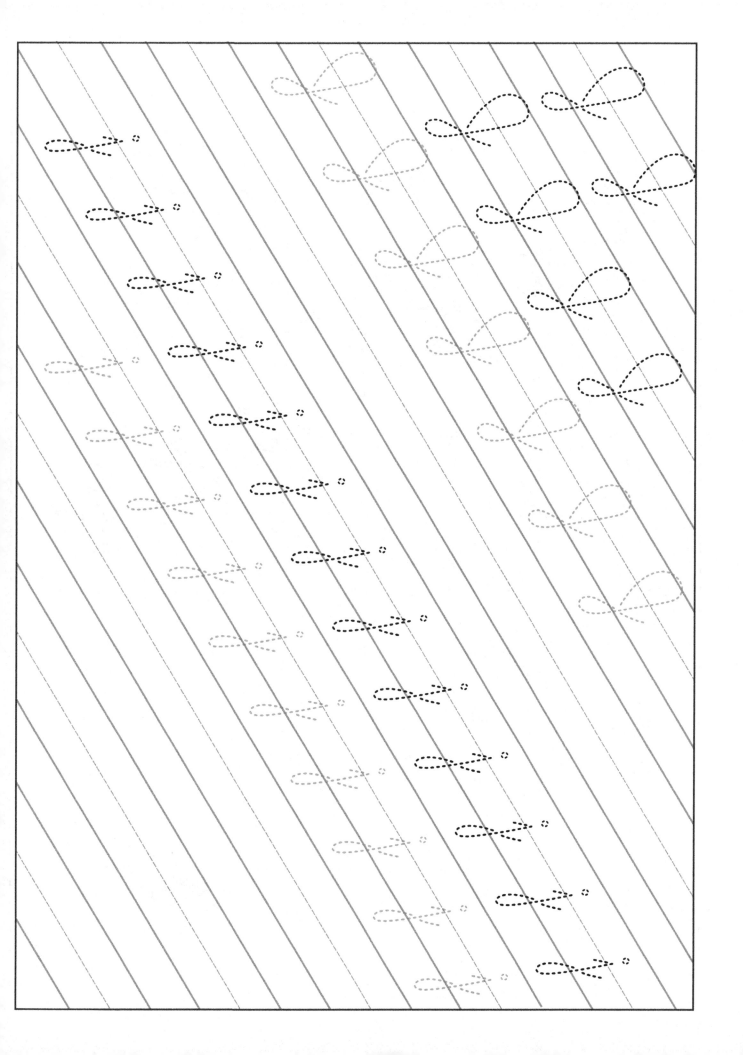

Trace the cursive letters, then write your own.

K is for Koala

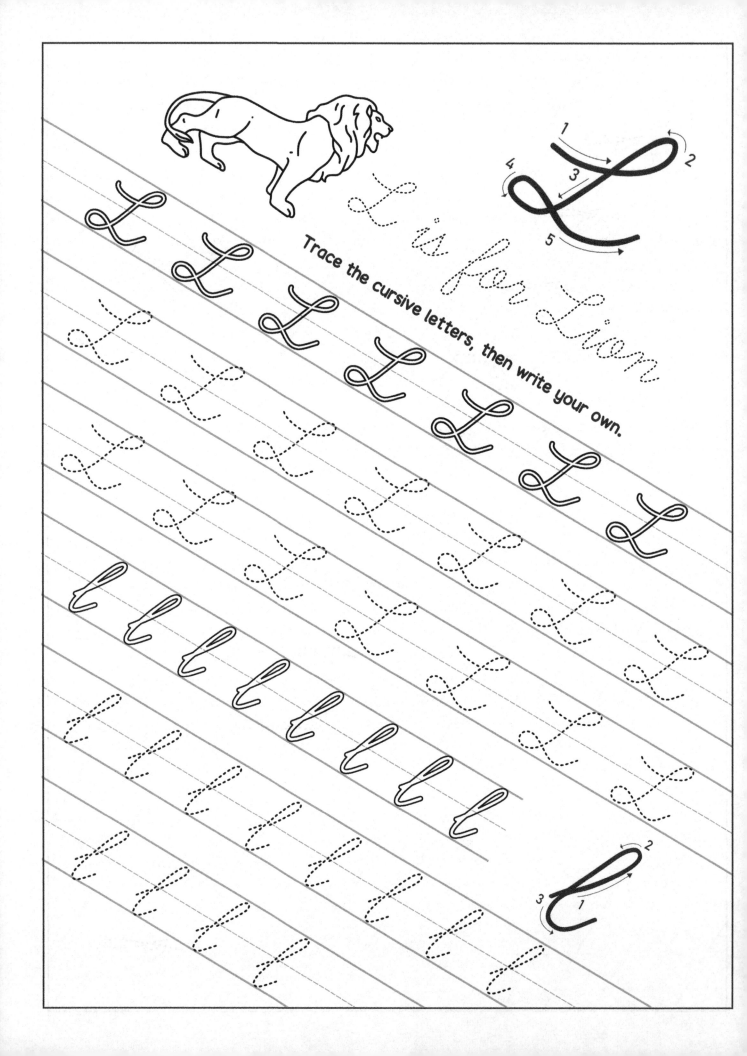

Trace the cursive letters, then write your own.

Trace the cursive letters, then write your own.

m is for mouse

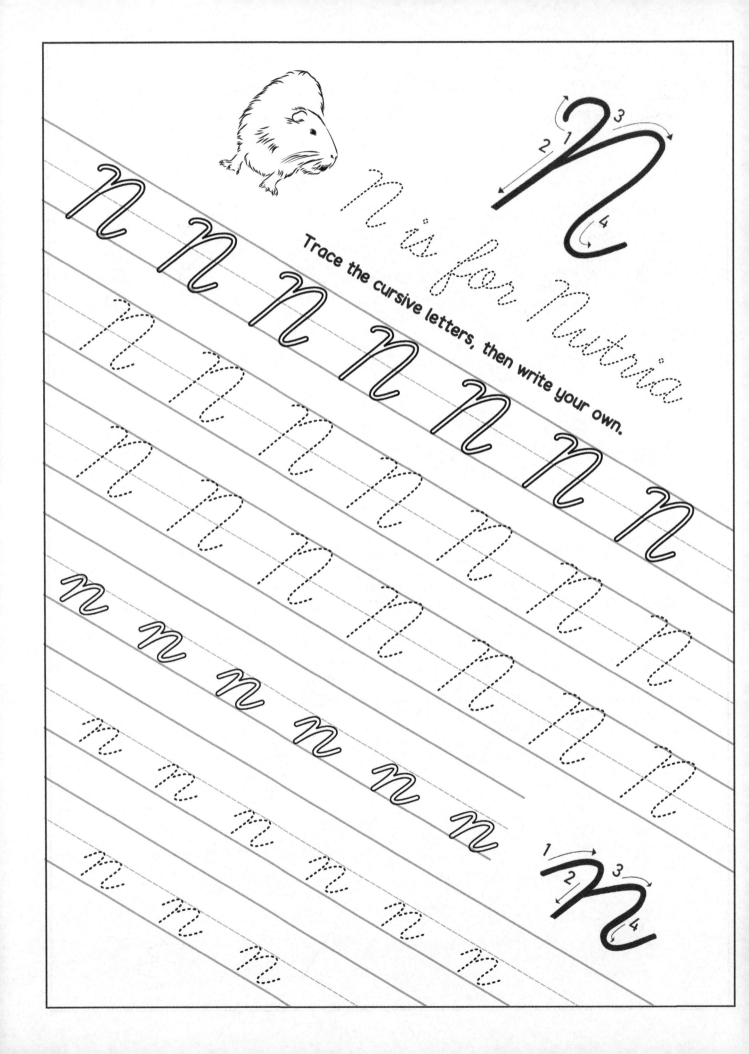

Trace the cursive letters, then write your own.

n is for nutria

Trace the cursive letters, then write your own.

O is for Ostrich

_p_ is for penguin

Trace the cursive letters, then write your own.

Trace the cursive letters, then write your own.

Trace the cursive letters, then write your own.

R is for Racoon

Trace the cursive letters, then write your own.

S is for sheep

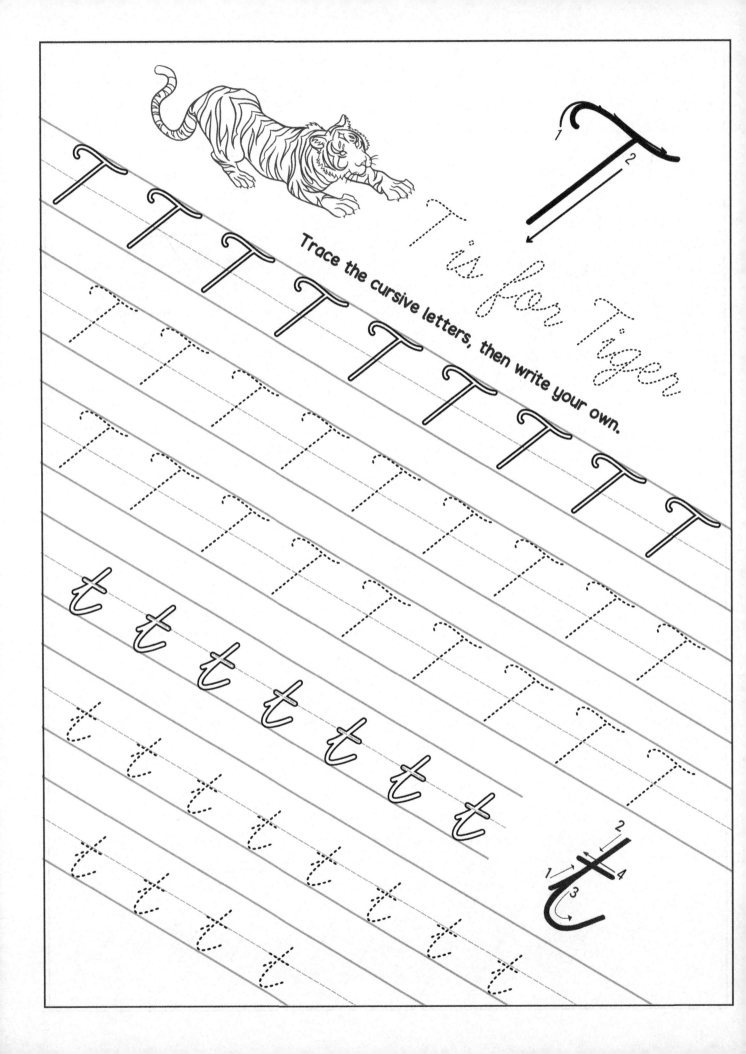

Trace the cursive letters, then write your own.

T is for Tiger

Trace the cursive letters, then write your own.

U is for *Urchin*

Trace the cursive letters, then write your own.

V is for Vulture

Trace the cursive letters, then write your own.

W is for walrus

Trace the cursive letters, then write your own.

x is for Xerus

Trace the cursive letters, then write your own.

Y is for yak

Trace the cursive letters, then write your own.

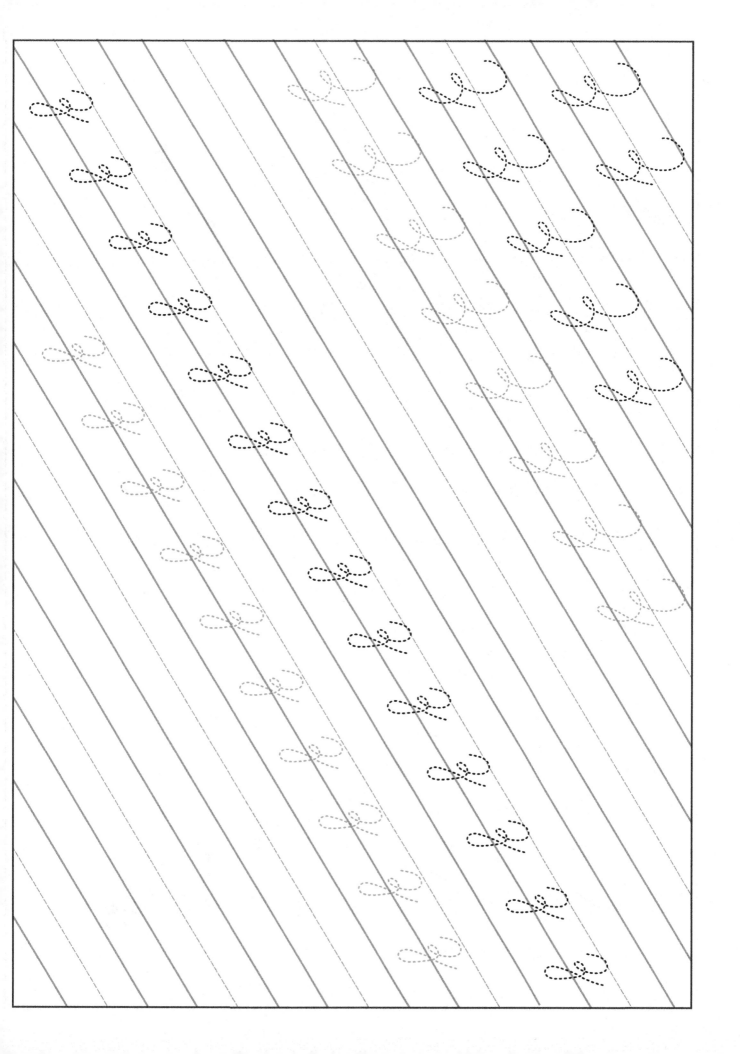

Trace the cursive letters, then write your own.

Trace the cursive letters, then write your own.

2 2 2 2 2 2 2 2

Two Two Two Two

Trace the cursive letters, then write your own.

Trace the cursive letters, then write your own.

Trace the cursive letters, then write your own.

5 5 5 5 5 5 5 5 5

Five Five Five

Five Five Five

Five

Trace the cursive letters, then write your own.

6 6 6 6 6 6 6

Six Six Six Six

Trace the cursive letters, then write your own.

Seven Seven Seven

Trace the cursive letters, then write your own.

Trace the cursive letters, then write your own.

Trace the cursive letters, then write your own.

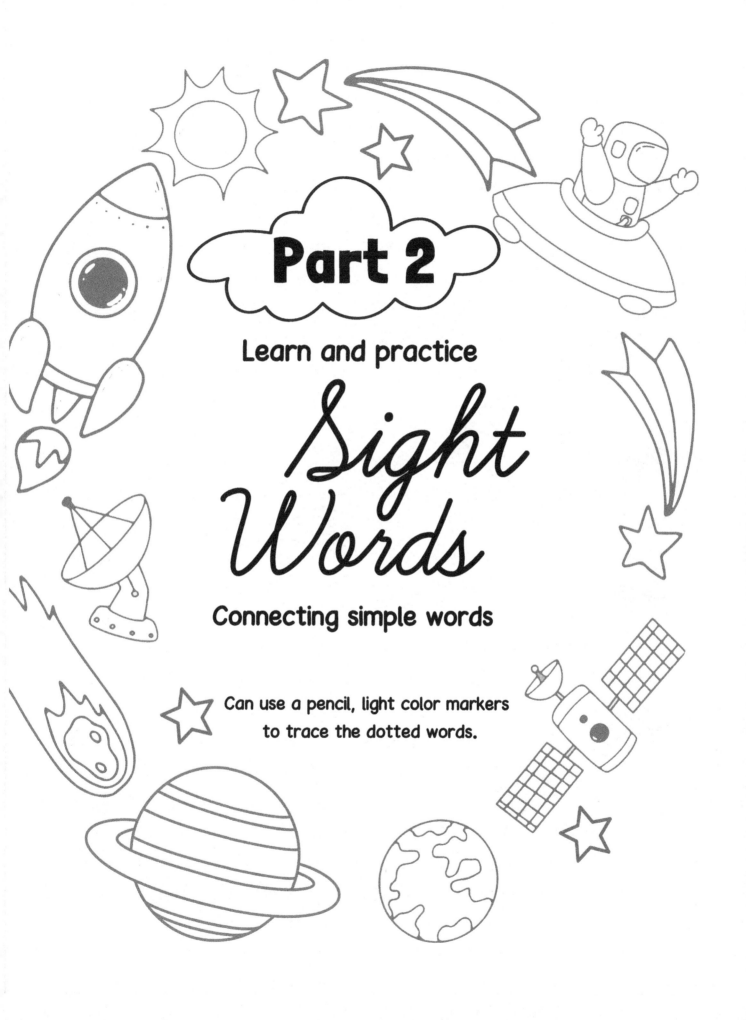

Part 2

Learn and practice

Sight Words

Connecting simple words

Can use a pencil, light color markers
to trace the dotted words.

and

big

can

dark

eat

away

best

ever

give

help

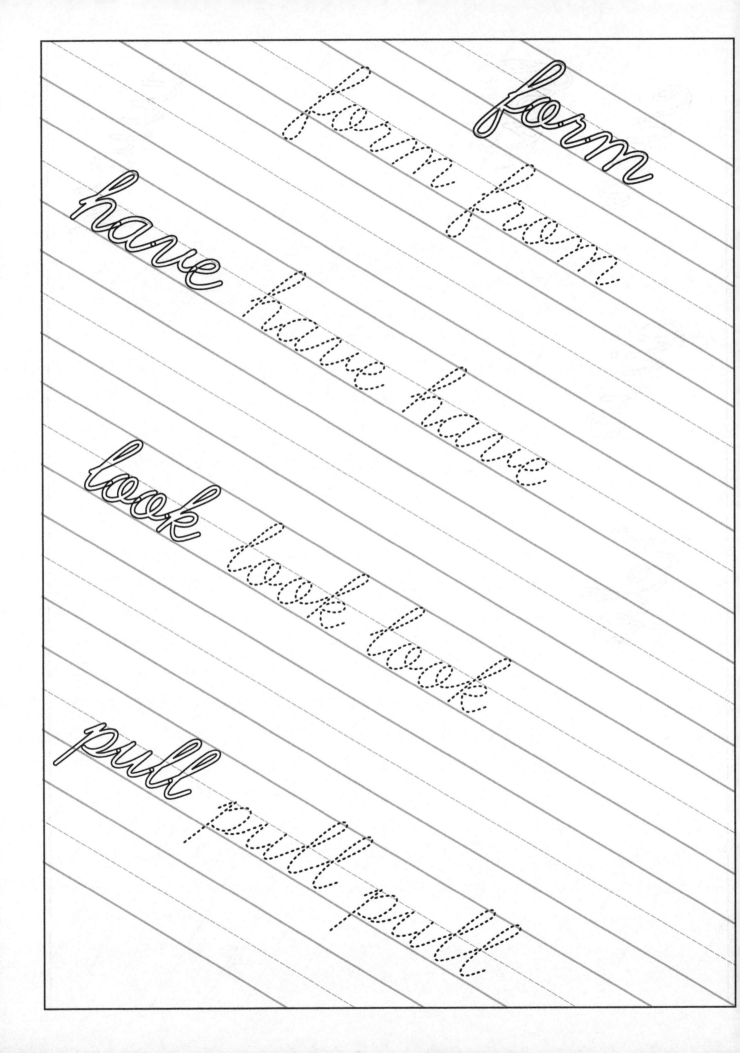

form

form form

have

have have have

look

look look look

pull

pull pull pull

again

begin

drink

think

there

better

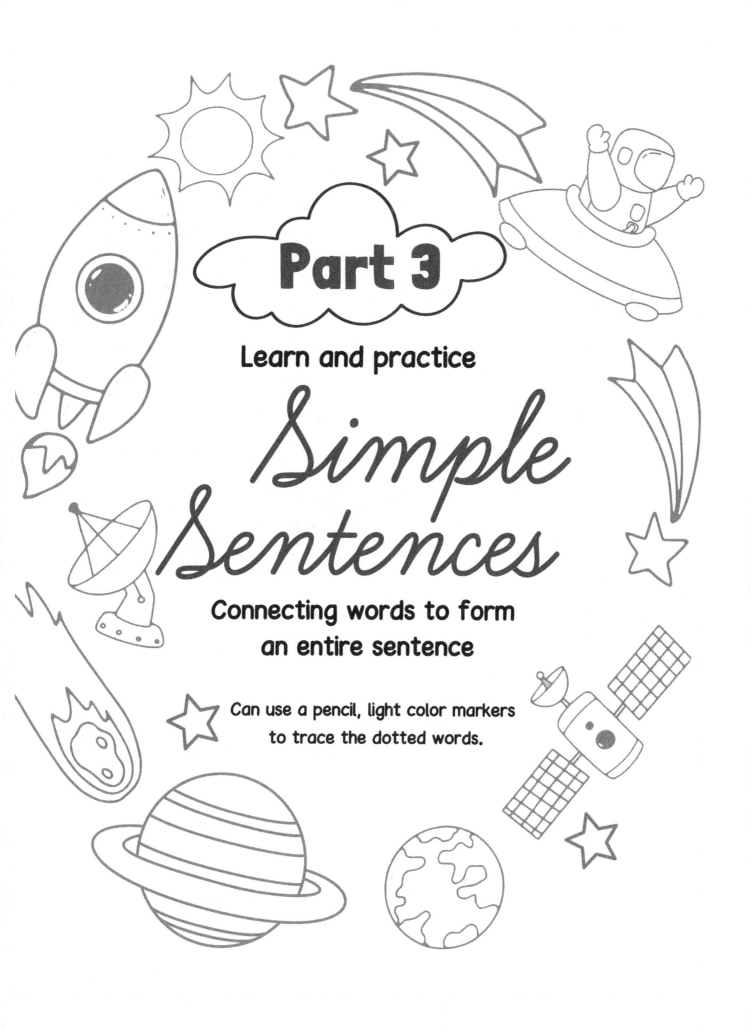

Part 3

Learn and practice

Simple Sentences

Connecting words to form
an entire sentence

Can use a pencil, light color markers
to trace the dotted words.

You are very brave.

I take a bite.

Let's hold hands.

Keep the dog out.

We need each other.

May I
use your toilet?

Lemons are sour.

Everybody loves her.

Trace the letters.

Butter is made from milk.

They will find you.

Nothing is easy.

I gave him a book.

It's

just a cold.

A square has four sides.

Nancy

trees fell down.

Summer is over.

Fry me some eggs.

Show me the photo.

Well begun is half done.

When is

your birthday?

Jack likes walking.

He is my best friend.

You are a doctor.

She learned to read by herself.

Made in United States
Orlando, FL
11 November 2024

53723994R00059